ESSENTIAL LIFE SKILLS SERIES

WHAT YOU NEED TO KNOW ABOUT

READING ADS, REFERENCE MATERIALS & LEGAL DOCUMENTS

Second Edition

Carolyn Morton Starkey   Norgina Wright Penn

National Textbook Company
NTC a division of *NTC Publishing Group* • Lincolnwood, Illinois USA

ACKNOWLEDGMENTS

Alberto-Culver Co., Bold Hold coupon

BMG Direct Marketing, Inc., RCA Music Service ad

Book-of-the-Month Club, Inc., offer

Buick Motor Division, General Motors Corp., warranty

J. G. Ferguson Publishing Co., *World Book Dictionary* entry

General Mills, Inc., Cheerios coupon

Globe Book Co., table of contents from Henry I. Christ, *Modern Short Biographies,* copyright © 1979, Globe Book Co., Inc.

Johnson Publishing Co., *Jet* subscription form; *Ebony* table of contents

Sears, Roebuck and Co., credit application

Sharp Electronics Corp., Sharp CB warranty

Starlog Magazine, contents page

Peter Fitzgerald for drawings on pages 3, 7, 8, 9

Preface

This revised edition from the Essential Life Skills Series tells you what you need to know about reading ads, legal documents, and reference materials. Mastering these reading skills will make you more assertive and self-confident. You will learn to cope better with everyday situations.

This book covers some familiar yet very important materials. You will learn to read and understand:

ads	library reference materials
special offers	dictionaries
credit agreements	tables of contents
warranties	indexes

Throughout the book you will find examples of real ads, credit agreements, warranties, and reference materials, like the ones you see and use every day.

Each section in this book includes definitions of words that may be new or difficult. Checkup sections help you review what you have learned. There are many opportunities to practice your skills.

Because of its flexible format, this book can be used either for self-study or in a group setting with an instructor. The answer key is on perforated pages so that it is easy to remove.

When you have mastered the skills in this book, you will want to develop other skills to become more successful in our modern world. The other books in the Essential Life Skills Series will show you how.

Essential Life Skills Series

What You Need to Know about Reading Labels, Directions & Newspapers 5655-2

What You Need to Know about Reading Ads, Reference Materials & Legal Documents 5656-0

What You Need to Know about Getting a Job and Filling Out Forms 5657-9

What You Need to Know about Reading Signs, Directories, Schedules, Maps, Charts & Utility Bills 5658-7

What You Need to Know about Basic Writing Skills, Letters & Consumer Complaints 5659-6

Contents

Reading critically

As a buyer, you see or hear many advertising messages each day. These messages urge you to buy an item because it is "on sale." Sometimes a special offer sounds "too good to be true." To spend your money wisely, you must be able to read these ads critically. You must also be able to evaluate special offers.

Advertisements

WORDS TO KNOW

bandwagon appeal   the suggestion that you should not miss out on something that lots of other people are doing or buying

consumer   any person who buys and uses up, or consumes, a product

endorse   to give approval, such as the famous football player advertising a well-known soft drink

imply   to suggest something that is not said; for example, implying that a beautiful appearance will lead to fame and fortune

glowing generality   a statement that says something is wonderful or great without giving proof; no specific information

guarantee   a promise of quality or length of use. Often the seller promises to fix or replace a product for a certain length of time.

optional   an extra feature, usually for an additional price

symbol   when one thing suggests something else, such as beautiful hair for happiness or a car for success

technique   a method or way of doing something

vanity   pride in yourself or your appearance

Do you read the ads in newspapers and magazines? Have you ever bought something simply because it was on sale? Have you ever bought a product because it was endorsed by a superstar? Advertisements are aimed at consumers. They try to make you spend your money. People do buy products because of ads they have seen.

There are many ways you can learn about a product. A friend could recommend a product to you. You could hear about a product at school or work. Sometimes you see something new and decide to buy it. However, most buyers learn about products through ads.

Makers of products spend millions of dollars a year in advertising. They want you to know what they have for sale. They reach you through television and radio commercials. They advertise in newspapers. They advertise in magazines and on billboards.

As a consumer, there are lots of things you need to know about the products you buy. This makes advertising important. Here are some of the things you can learn from ads:

- What an item costs
- What it looks like
- What features it has
- Where you can get it
- How long it can be gotten
- Who makes it
- How it compares to other brands
- Whether it's guaranteed

This type of information is important to you. Sometimes advertisers forget this. They may be advertising a good product, but they don't tell you much about it. Instead, they try to get your attention in other ways. Some advertisers need to use these techniques to sell their product. They know their product is not a famous brand name. They know the product may lack quality. And they know it may not have sales appeal. There are other advertisers who use these techniques simply because they work.

Many makers of products hire trained people to write their ads. Ad firms use talented people—artists, photographers, writers—to think up ads that will appeal to you. They create ads that they hope will make you want to buy a product. You may see a movie star holding up a jar of "Crunchy Nut" Peanut Butter. You may buy this peanut butter just because of the famous person. Children are also targets for ads, especially television ads. TV commercials coach children to ask their parents for "Fruity-Froot" cereal. They want "Fruity-Froot" because (1) it comes with a toy whistle, (2) it's chocolate coated, and (3) it's the brand "Super Hero" eats. The point is this: All ads try to make you buy a product. Many of these things you may want, need, and can afford. But there are other products that ads make you want. You may not need these things.

As a buyer, you must learn to judge ads. You must watch out for advertising techniques. You must learn to look for the facts about what you are buying.

Here are some things you should know about ads in general:

1. *Some ads lie.* The seller or maker of a product simply does not tell the truth about the product.
2. *Some ads tell half the truth.* This type of advertising misleads the buyer. The ad will *suggest* that something is true. An ad may say just enough to make you say the rest. Sometimes the ad may tell you only half of what you need to know.
3. *Some ads will appeal to your emotions:*
   - your desire to look and feel younger (or older), sexy, handsome
   - your identification with family, friend, country, a TV star
   - memories of "down home" and "the good ol' days"
   - your need to be part of the crowd
4. *Some ads are filled with glowing generalities.* These ads tell you that a product is WONDERFUL, GREAT, FANTASTIC, SUPER, BETTER THAN EVER!
5. *Some ads appeal to your senses,* especially touch and taste. "Cotton Cloud" Soap makes your towels feel soft and fluffy. "Lemon-Lime Lemonade" tastes "lemony," "limey," and delicious!

Lies and half-truths

It's hard to know if some ads tell the truth. The claims made sound good. The ads are *believable*. This is why many consumer groups go after advertisers who print misleading ads. There are now laws that make advertisers tell you more about products. It is too bad that most people learn that an ad has misled them only after they have bought and used a product. Jan used Dawn's Magic Beauty Cream for three weeks. But she could not get rid of her freckles. Tommy Madison threw out his Body Tone FLEX-erciser. After two weeks he hadn't lost the eight inches of fat the ad said he'd lose. And Sarah Hart put her trust in M-24 Special Formula Mouth Wash. She may never know it doesn't help fight colds.

It's even harder to point out the half-truths. A mail-order school might say that it helps its graduates find jobs. It doesn't say that it directs graduates to the local newspaper. A record club may promise you FOUR HIT RECORDS FREE. If you read the ad closely, you learn that you have to buy four albums to keep the four FREE ones.

Activity 1

Reading ads — lies and half-truths

Answer the questions about the following ads.

LOSE FAT FOREVER

BEFORE   AFTER

You Can Look Like This!

BUY **Fat Off**

No pills, no exercise, no diet.

Fat Off approved by doctors and health clinics.

1. List all the information in this ad that you feel is not true or is only half true.

_____

_____

2. List all the information in this ad that you feel is true (fact).

_____

_____

GET A CAREER CERTIFICATE

TRAIN AT HOME!!!!!!

You don't need a high school diploma or an equivalency diploma (GED)—

JUST SIGN UP TODAY

OUR GRADUATES EARN

UP TO **$50,000**

Each course is a full semester. You don't have to pay now!
ENROLL NOW FOR THIS SEMESTER!!!
Just check the home-study course of your choice. Enclose a $10 registration fee.
Begin your training in JUST 2 WEEKS.

- -

☐ TYPING   ☐ TRUCK DRIVING   ☐ CATERING   ☐ COMPUTER PROGRAMING
☐ AUTO MECHANICS ☐ HAIR STYLING   ☐ BARBERING   ☐ DRIVER INSTRUCTOR
                                                     TRAINING

GET YOUR CAREER CERTIFICATE TODAY!!!

I have enclosed $10 for my registration fee. You will bill me later
for tuition. I can choose a convenient payment plan.

I have enclosed a   ☐ Check   ☐ Money Order

Signature _____ Date_____
        (Sign your name in ink)

CAREER CERTIFICATES, Box 80A, Trainingsville, USA

- -

*** HURRY ***

**************** DON'T MISS THIS OPPORTUNITY TO TRAIN AT HOME ****************

START YOUR NEW CAREER TODAY!

1. Does this ad give you the name of the school? _____

2. Does this ad give you a street address (and a building) or just a box number? _____

3. List the home study courses being offered.

_____

_____

_____

4. Which of these courses would probably be best taught in a school with an instructor? Explain.

_____

_____

_____

_____

5. Which of these people would probably answer this ad?

_____ a retired person _____ a high school graduate with no vocational skills

_____ a college graduate _____ an adult who never attended high school

_____ a high school drop out

6. Which of these things does the ad *imply* (make you think something is true without actually saying it)? More than one response is possible.

_____ When you finish the course, your "Career Certificate" will help you get a job.

_____ Many people who take a career course earn $50,000 a year.

_____ If you are not happy with the course, you will get your money back.

_____ Your $10 will be refunded if you change your mind in the two weeks before the course begins.

_____ Typing is a better career choice than catering.

_____ You don't have to worry about money now. The important thing is to enroll for the current semester. You can always pay later.

_____ The training is like college. (There are semesters, registration, tuition fees.)

Emotional appeals

Many ads appeal to your emotions. Some ads may appeal to your vanity. They tell you that you'll look beautiful ... young ... sexy ... handsome.... Some ads will touch things dear to you: "Have you talked to your family lately? Call them long distance. It only costs a few pennies." Or "Every American should take stock in America. Buy bonds." Family, friends, country, the flag—all are things that bring out emotions in people. And of course there are strong feelings about things past: homemade goodness, down-home flavor, memories of childhood.

Activity 2

Reading ads with emotional appeal

Each of the ads below appeals to your emotions. Is it your vanity? . . . your intelligence? . . . your good looks? Answer the questions about each ad.

INTELLIGENT
SHOPPERS. . .

BUY

SUPER SHINE

FURNITURE POLISH

They've compared brands-
They know **SUPER SHINE**
outshines them all!

What does this ad appeal

to?____
(a) Your need to feel your house is clean
(b) Your need to feel smart
(c) Your vanity

Feel beautiful. . .
Look beautiful. . .
Be beautiful. . .

USE

Hair Color Magic

The shampoo and hair color for the beautiful you. . .

What does this ad appeal

to?____
(a) Your need to belong
(b) Your intelligence
(c) Your vanity

Activity 3

Reading ads with emotional appeal — "the famous person"

An ad that has a lot of emotional appeal is the famous person ad. Sometimes your favorite television star will endorse a product. You like this person. You are a loyal fan. You transfer your emotions for the person to the product. If "Ron Tramolta" eats it, wears it, or drinks it, you will too. Maybe if you use Pep-so-Tent toothpaste, you'll have white, attractive teeth like "Teenie Turnie." The next ad is a famous person ad. Answer the questions about this ad.

1. Why do you think this famous person was asked to do this ad? _____

2. This ad is filled with OPINIONS—what a person *thinks* about the product. List all the opinions you

   find in this ad. _____

3. Which of the following statements best summarizes this ad? _____
   (a) Dick Fetty uses PST in his car, and you should use it in yours.
   (b) Whatever is good for Dick Fetty's car is good for everybody's car because he's a famous race driver.
   (c) PST will make your car run well enough for the Indiana 600.

Activity 4

Reading ads with emotional appeal — "get on the bandwagon"

Some ads appeal to your need to follow the crowd. Many people call this the bandwagon ad. The ad makes you feel left out—not in with what everyone else is doing. Read the following ad carefully. Then answer the questions about it.

1. List all the words and phrases that appeal to a person's desire to join the crowd. _____

_____

2. How does this ad use *art* to help convince you that you should "get on the bandwagon"? _____

_____

3. Do you think that buying something because everyone else seems to be is a good reason? Explain why

you feel the way you do. _____

Glowing generalities

When you read an ad, you should expect to find out more about a product. Has the brand been tested? If so, by whom? What is being said? Are there facts that can be checked out? How does the product compare to other brands? What does it cost? How long does it last? Sometimes, instead of facts, ads contain a lot of general statements. If all the generalities were taken out of the ad, you would find that the ad told you very little, if anything, about the product.

Activity 5

Reading ads — specific information or glowing generality?

Read the following ad and the statements from this ad. Do these statements contain specific information or glowing generalities?

THE NEW FLEETLINE
THE CAR OF THE FUTURE

- ▶ Improved steering
- ▶ More space than ever
- ▶ V-8 engine
- ▶ Vinyl roof
- ▶ Air conditioning
- ▶ Tremendous mileage

Now is the time for spectacular savings on this year's spectacular car. You have a variety of options and colors to choose from. You have a chance to ride the most sensational automobile on the road, the Fleetline—Tomorrow's car—today.

	Specific information	Glowing generality
1. The Fleetline has a V-8 engine.	_____	_____
2. The Fleetline gives you tremendous mileage.	_____	_____
3. This car has "more space than ever."	_____	_____
4. The Fleetline comes with a vinyl roof.	_____	_____
5. The Fleetline comes in a variety of colors.	_____	_____
6. The Fleetline is this year's spectacular car.	_____	_____

9

CHECK YOUR UNDERSTANDING OF ADVERTISEMENTS

Here are some words you should know when you are reading ads critically. Find the correct word for each of the statements below.

guarantee	endorse	vanity
bandwagon appeal	optional	glowing generality

1. My new watch came with a _____ against defects for six months.

2. The ad for skin cream says that your skin will feel great after using the cream. This statement is

a _____ .

3. Ads for certain kinds of sweaters or jackets appeal to a person's _____ .

4. Ads for certain products say that since so many other people are buying the product, you should,

too. This is called a _____ .

5. Certain features, like air conditioning, are _____ on a new car.

6. During baseball season, famous players often _____ certain products.

List the advertising technique used in each of the following quotations from ads. Refer to p. 2 for a list of the advertising techniques you have been studying.

7. "Driving is a new sensation . . . America's most popular sports car. Hot stuff." _____

8. "Don't miss this wonderful product." _____

9. "Lose 10 pounds in one week without dieting!" _____

10. "Sheets that are soft, smooth, fragrant." _____

Special offers

The consumer's world is filled with sales offers. Many offers are found in newspapers and magazines. Others come to you in the mail. These special offers can mean savings to you. You must read these offers very carefully. How much of a savings will you get? What will your responsibilities be?

Reading magazine subscription offers

With a subscription you can get magazines through the mail at discount prices. Magazine subscriptions are often for one or two years. Sometimes magazines have special offers for short periods. These offers give very low prices. They are for *new* subscribers. A subscriber's rate will be below the newsstand price.

When you read subscription offers, there are three things you want to know: (1) how long your subscription will last (or how many issues you will get), (2) what the subscription will cost, and (3) how much of a savings you will get.

Activity 6

Interpreting magazine subscription offers

Read the following magazine subscription offer. Decide whether the statements about the offer are TRUE (T) or FALSE (F).

FOR THE 52 WEEKS OF CHRISTMAS

The one Christmas gift that's always the right size, shape, color and price.

An Attractive Card Announces Your Gift

First one-year subscription $24.00
Each additional subscription $20.00.
Offer Good in United States Only

Your Name_____
Please Print

Address_____ Apt. #_____

City_____

State_____ Zip_____

_____My own order   _____Renewal with Gifts

Payment Enclosed $_____   Bill me_____

Mail To: JET Gift Subscriptions, 820 South Michigan Ave., Chicago, Illinois 60605

Name_____
Please Print

Address_____ Apt. #_____

City_____

State_____ Zip_____

Gift Card From_____

Name_____
Please Print

Address_____ Apt. #_____

City_____

State_____ Zip_____

Gift Card From_____

Name_____
Please Print

Address_____ Apt. #_____

City_____

State_____ Zip_____

Gift Card From_____

_____ **1.** This is a weekly magazine.

_____ **2.** You may have a gift card sent with gift subscriptions.

_____ **3.** Your first subscription will cost $24.00.

_____ **4.** Each additional subscription will cost $20.00.

_____ **5.** Canadians can take advantage of this offer for a slightly higher cost.

Reading record and tape club offers

Record and tape club memberships appeal to both teenagers and adults. These offers require special reading skills. You may be able to save money on records, tapes, or even compact discs. To get the special prices, however, you usually must agree to make more purchases.

When you read these offers, read for specific details. Know how many more purchases you have to make. Read to understand what kind of discount, if any, you will get as a member. Know what kind of musical choices you will have. Will you be able to select classical music? country? pop? hard rock? Read to find out what you must do if you ever want to cancel your membership. All this information should be somewhere in the membership offer. It is up to you to read for the specific details of the offer.

Activity 7

Reading record and tape club offers for details

Read the record and tape offer on the next page. Then answer the questions below.

1. How much must you send to join the RCA Music Service? _____

2. How often will you receive offers of main selections? _____ of special selections? _____

3. If you want the main selection, what do you do? _____

4. If you want an alternate record or tape, what do you do? _____

5. How many days do you have to make your choice? _____

6. If you receive a record or tape before this time, can it be returned? _____

7. Will you get full credit? _____

8. Who pays shipping charges? _____

9. What is the regular club price for records or tapes? _____ the special sales price? _____

   the price for compact discs? _____

10. When can you cancel your membership? _____

14

Book club membership offers are a lot like record and tape club offers. Best sellers, like hit records, are offered to new members at special low prices. Once you accept a membership offer, you must purchase a certain number of books within a certain amount of time. You may have six months to make these purchases. Sometimes you may have as long as a year. You must read carefully for the specific details of the offer. Know what you're agreeing to do.

Activity 8

Read this book club offer. Answer the questions about this offer.

Reading a
book club offer
for details

Choose any 4 for $2.

You simply agree to buy 4 books within the next two years.

Book-of-the-Month Club, Inc., Camp Hill, Pennsylvania 17012   A304-10-1

Please enroll me as a member of Book-of-the-Month Club and send me the 4 books I've listed below, billing me $2, plus shipping and handling charges. I agree to buy 4 more books during the next two years. A shipping and handling charge is added to each shipment.

Indicate by number the four books you want

Mr.
Mrs.   2-04
Miss _____ (Please print plainly)

Address_____ Apt _____

City_____

State_____ Zip_____

Prices generally higher in Canada

BOOK-OF-THE-MONTH CLUB
America's Bookstore® since 1926.

Benefits of Membership. Membership in the Book-of-the-Month Club begins with your choice of 4 of today's best books for $2. Because our prices are generally lower than the publishers' prices, you will save throughout your membership on the finest new titles. In fact, the longer you remain a member, the greater your savings can be. Our Book-Dividend® plan, for which you become eligible after a brief trial enrollment, offers savings from 50% to 75% off the publishers' prices on art books, reference works, classics, books on cooking and crafts, literary sets and other contemporary works of enduring value. Nevertheless, all Book-of-the-Month Club books are equal in quality to the publishers' originals; they are not condensed versions or cheaply made reprints.

As a member you will receive the *Book-of-the-Month Club News®* 15 times a year (about every 3½ weeks). Every issue reviews a Selection and 150 other books that we call Alternates, which are carefully chosen by our editors. If you want the Selection, do nothing. It will be shipped to you automatically. If you want one or more Alternates—or no book at all—indicate your decision on the Reply Form and return it by the specified date. *Return Privilege:* If the *News* is delayed and you receive the Selection without having had 10 days to notify us, you may return it for credit at our expense. *Cancellations:* Membership may be discontinued, either by you or by the Club, at any time after you have bought 4 additional books. Join today. With savings and choices like these, no wonder Book-of-the-Month Club is America's Bookstore.

1. If Book-of-the-Month Club accepts your application, how many books will you receive? _____

2. What will these books cost? _____

3. How many days do you have to decide if you want to keep the main selection? _____

4. If you accept the books, are there any other charges? _____

5. How often will you receive the Book-of-the-Month Club news? _____

6. By accepting this offer, how many books are you agreeing to buy during the next two years? _____

7. If you do not want the Selection of the Month, what do you do? _____

Coupon savings   Many ads have savings coupons. You can use these discount coupons for savings on a lot of products. First, you clip the coupon out. You then redeem it at the time of your purchase. Some coupons will be for refunds. To get a refund you usually have to show proof-of-purchase. Proof-of-purchase can be a label, a price code, or a cash register receipt. Shopping with coupons can result in savings. Sometimes there's something FREE with your purchase. However, coupons are still a form of advertising. Read all coupons carefully. Sometimes a savings may not be on a product you need. Coupons have expiration dates, too. You must use a coupon before it expires.

Activity 9

Reading coupon offers

Answer the questions about the following coupon offers.

1. What two products can you buy with these coupons? _____

_____

2. Do you have to buy a certain size? _____

3. Can you redeem these coupons for cash without making a purchase? _____

4. Do these coupons have expiration dates? _____

16

CHECK YOUR UNDERSTANDING OF SPECIAL OFFERS

Here are some words to know when you are reading a special offer. Find the correct word or phrase for each of the sentences below.

redeem   coupon   expiration date

discount   refund   obligation

1. A _____ for 10¢ off on the price of crackers was in the daily newspaper.

2. The _____ of the coupon was March 31, 1989.

3. When I joined a book club, I had a(n) _____ to purchase 4 additional books.

4. The electronic toy I purchased included a coupon for a $5 _____ .

5. I like to buy things at _____ stores because they offer products at lower prices.

6. I decided to buy a certain brand of crackers because I had a coupon to _____ .

Decide whether the following statements are TRUE (T) or FALSE (F).

_____ **7.** When a book club offers a number of books for an introductory low price, you can get these books without buying anything else from the club at that time.

_____ **8.** Record and tape and book clubs usually automatically send you the selection of the month.

_____ **9.** Magazine and newspaper subscriptions cost less than the newsstand price.

_____ **10.** Coupons for food products never have expiration dates.

Under-standing agreements and warranties

Have you ever returned an item for a refund, leased a piece of equipment, or made a credit card purchase? Chapter 5 explores consumer agreements and contracts and the warranties that come with certain purchases. You will study sales and service agreements. You will also study credit agreements. You will interpret the terms used in these agreements. This chapter presents a number of warranties for your review. It includes a cassette player warranty and a new car warranty.

Agreements and contracts

WORDS TO KNOW

annual   each year

balance   the amount you owe after payment; amount left

collateral   property promised to a creditor, such as a car or furniture, if a debt is not paid

co-maker   second person agreeing to credit terms; also co-applicant, co-signer, or co-borrower

conditions   terms; special circumstances

contract   legal agreement

consent   agree to; give permission

consumer   buyer or borrower

credit   ability to buy or borrow and pay at a later date

credit terms   how you are to pay for a credit purchase or repay a loan

creditor   person or business giving you credit; lender; seller

debts   bills you owe; obligations

default   nonpayment; failure to pay as agreed

delinquent   late

disclosure to make known; to state in writing; a written statement of the terms of a loan or credit agreement

down payment money paid in advance on credit purchase

entitle give the right to; permit; allow

finance charge cost of having credit; monthly charge on credit agreement, usually used on charge card agreements

installment monthly payment

interest cost of credit, usually used in loan agreements

landlord person who owns and rents out a house, apartment, or building

lease a rent agreement

liability legal responsibility

lien a legal claim on your property for nonpayment of a debt

option choice

percentage rate interest or finance charges stated as a percent of what you owe

retailer seller or merchant; person or business giving credit

sue take to court

tenant person renting an apartment, a house, or a building

title legal document proving ownership

violate fail to keep an agreement

The special words used for contracts and agreements are very technical. You will see these words in credit agreements. You will see them in rent agreements. You will see them in employment agency contracts, too. You will also see these words in sales and service agreements. For example, retail stores often post rules about returns and refunds. There may be terms on the receipt of your car repair bill. There may be terms on the back of your dry-cleaning ticket. (Dry cleaners take very little responsibility for damaged clothes.) Some of these agreements do not require your signature. But they are still agreements. When you buy goods or pay for services, you are accepting the terms of the seller. Study the *Words to Know* carefully. They are the words you will see and use. Your understanding of them can help you protect your rights.

Activity 1

Using credit terms

The words below are often found in credit agreements. Use these words to complete the statements below.

disclosure	percentage rate	debts
co-maker	delinquent	default
creditor	interest	installment
down payment		

1. Ira Atkins just got a(n) _____ loan for a new car.

2. Of course, Ira will have to pay _____ on this loan.

3. The annual _____ is stated in the credit agreement.

4. Ira had to read a _____ statement before signing the credit agreement.

5. The _____ must always let you know the terms of credit.

6. There was a _____ required.

7. Ira's wife, Ellen, was _____ of the loan.

8. Ellen will have to repay the loan should Ira _____ .

9. The _____ charges are $5 per month for each late payment.

10. When Ira and Ellen applied for the loan, they had to list all their _____ .

Activity 2

Reading credit agreements

Each of the statements below was taken from a credit agreement. The language is very technical. Which of the statements given means the same as the statement from the agreement?

1.
> If an installment is not paid within 10 days after it is due, a delinquent charge of $5 will be paid by the buyer . . .

_____ a. If you are late with your monthly payment, you must pay $5.

_____ b. If you are more than 10 days late with a payment, you must pay a "late charge."

_____ c. If you are more than 10 days late with your monthly payment, you must pay $5 in late charges.

2.

> For the purpose of securing payment of the obligation, creditor holds title to 1982 Buick as collateral and shall have a security interest in said property until said obligation is fully paid . . .

_____ a. Your title will be held until you pay your debt.
_____ b. You can hold the title to your property, but if you fail to pay this bill, the lender will demand the title to your car.
_____ c. To be sure you pay this bill, the lender will hold the ownership papers to your car until the bill is paid in full.

3.

> Debtor will not sell or offer to sell or otherwise transfer ownership of the collateral without written consent of creditor . . .

_____ a. You can't sell the collateral, for example, a car.
_____ b. The lender can sell or transfer the collateral (car) if he lets you know in writing.
_____ c. As the borrower, you can't sell the collateral (car) unless the person holding the collateral or title to the collateral gives you written permission.

4.

> As co-signer of this agreement, I am aware of my liability and I hereby authorize you to obtain credit information relative to me.

_____ a. As co-maker of a loan, you are responsible for the loan if it is not paid.
_____ b. You have agreed to share the responsibility for a debt.
_____ c. You have signed to have your credit checked and to share the responsibility for a debt.

Activity 3

Using agreements and contract words

Match the words on the left with their meanings on the right.

_____ A. lease	1. failure to pay as agreed
_____ B. balance	2. amount you owe
_____ C. consumer	3. rent agreement
_____ D. entitle	4. terms
_____ E. landlord	5. buy-now and pay-later plan
_____ F. default	6. yearly
_____ G. obligation	7. buyer
_____ H. annual	8. allow
_____ I. credit	9. apartment owner
_____ J. conditions	10. responsibility

Activity 4

Reading terms on charge accounts

Many people make purchases by using credit cards or opening charge accounts. The law requires that *all* creditors provide buyers with disclosure information. This means companies offering charge accounts must give you the terms of your agreement in writing. This information will come with your application for credit. Sometimes it is separate from the application. When you put your signature on a credit agreement, you are accepting all of the terms in the agreement. This Sears Charge Account Agreement appears on the *back* of a Sears Charge Application.

Answer TRUE (T) or FALSE (F) to the following statements about the Sears credit terms.

_____ 1. You will not have to pay finance charges if you make regular monthly installment payments.

_____ 2. Payments must be made within 30 days of the billing date.

_____ 3. If your average daily balance is $28.50, the finance charge is 50¢.

_____ 4. If you make a $10 charge purchase on March 2 and a $150 charge on March 28, your finance charge for the month of March will be based on an average daily balance that does include the $150.

_____ 5. When you pay 1.75% in finance charges each month, you are paying 21% in finance charges each year.

_____ 6. You must pay the minimum payment each month.

_____ 7. You may pay more than the minimum monthly payment, but not less.

_____ 8. If you owe $210, your monthly payment will be $13.

_____ 9. Your signature gives Sears permission to investigate your credit record.

_____ 10. Unpaid finance or insurance charges are included when an average daily balance is figured.

SEARS, ROEBUCK AND CO.
SEARSCHARGE SECURITY AGREEMENT

On all charges to my SearsCharge account, I agree to the following:

1. **OPTION TO PAY IN FULL EACH MONTH TO AVOID FINANCE CHARGES.** I have the right each month to pay the total balance on my account. If I do so within 30 days (28 days for February statements) of my billing date, no **Finance Charge** will be added to the account for that month. The billing date will be shown on a statement sent to me each month. The total balance on my billing date will be called the New Balance on my monthly statement.

2. **OPTION TO PAY INSTALLMENTS PLUS A FINANCE CHARGE.** If I do not pay the total balance in full each month, I agree to make at least a minimum payment within 30 days (28 days for February statements) of the billing date shown on my monthly statement. The minimum payment required each month is shown in the Schedule of Minimum Monthly Payments below.

3. **SCHEDULE OF MINIMUM MONTHLY PAYMENTS.** The required minimum monthly payment is based on the highest New Balance on the account.

When the Highest New Balance Reaches:	The Minimum Monthly Payment will be:
$ .01 to $ 10.00	Balance
10.01 to 160.00	$10.00
160.01 to 180.00	11.00
180.01 to 200.00	12.00
200.01 to 220.00	13.00
220.01 to 240.00	14.00
240.01 to 260.00	15.00
260.01 to 290.00	16.00
290.01 to 340.00	17.00
340.01 to 380.00	18.00
380.01 to 410.00	19.00
410.01 to 440.00	20.00
440.01 to 470.00	21.00
470.01 to 500.00	22.00

You may always pay more than the required minimum monthly payment. The minimum payment will change only if charges to the account increase the balance to a new high. The minimum payment will not decrease until the New Balance is paid in full.

over $500.00 - 1/23rd of Highest Account Balance rounded to next higher whole dollar amount.

4. **FINANCE CHARGE.** If I do not pay the entire New Balance within 30 days (28 days for February statements) of the monthly billing date, a **Finance Charge** will be added to the account for the current monthly billing period. The *FINANCE CHARGE* will be either a minimum of 50¢ if the Average Daily Balance is $28.50 or less, or a periodic rate of 1.75% per month *(ANNUAL PERCENTAGE RATE of 21%)* on the Average Daily Balance.

5. **HOW TO DETERMINE THE AVERAGE DAILY BALANCE.** Sears will determine each day's outstanding balance in the monthly billing period and divide the total of these daily balances by the number of days in the monthly billing period. The result is the Average Daily Balance. Sears will include the current month's charges but will not include unpaid Finance or Insurance Charge(s), if any, when determining a daily balance. All payments and other credits will be subtracted from the previous day's balance.

6. **FAILURE TO MAKE MINIMUM PAYMENT.** If I do not make at least the minimum required monthly payment when due, Sears may declare my entire balance immediately due and payable.

7. **SECURITY INTEREST IN GOODS.** Sears has a security interest under the Uniform Commercial Code in all merchandise charged to the account. If I do not make payments as agreed, the security interest allows Sears to repossess only the merchandise which has not been paid in full. Upon my default, Sears may charge me reasonable attorneys' fees. I am responsible for any loss or damage to the merchandise until the price is fully paid. Any payments I make will first be used to pay any unpaid Insurance or Finance Charge(s), and then to pay for the earliest charges on the account. If more than one item is charged on the same date, my payment will apply first to the lowest priced item.

8. **CHANGE OF TERMS — CANCELLATION.** Sears has the right to change any terms or part of this agreement by sending me a written notice. Sears also has the right to cancel this agreement as it relates to future purchases. I agree to return all credit cards to Sears upon notice of such cancellation.

9. **STATE OF RESIDENCE CONTROLS TERMS.** All terms of this agreement are controlled by the laws of my state of residence.

10. **CHANGE OF RESIDENCE.** If I change my residence, I will inform Sears. Sears has the right to transfer the account to a unit servicing my new residence. If I move to another state, the account, including any unpaid balance, will be controlled by the credit terms which apply to Sears credit customers in my new state of residence. Sears will provide me with a written disclosure of any new terms, including the amount and method of calculating the **Finance Charge.**

11. **AUTHORIZED BUYERS.** This agreement controls all charges made on the account by me or any person I authorize to use the account.

12. **CREDIT INVESTIGATION AND DISCLOSURE.** Sears has the right to investigate my credit, employment and income records, and has the right to verify my credit references and to report the way I pay this account to credit bureaus and other interested parties.

13. **WAIVER OF LIEN ON DWELLING.** Sears gives up any right to retain or acquire any lien which Sears might be automatically entitled to by law on my principal dwelling. This does not apply to a lien created by a court judgment or acquired by a filing as provided by statute.

14. **ACCOUNT SUBJECT TO APPROVAL OF SEARS CREDIT SALES DEPARTMENT.** This agreement and all charges on the account are subject to the approval of Sears Credit Sales Department. The agreement will be considered approved when Sears delivers a Sears credit card or other notice of approval to me.

15. **ASSIGNMENT OF ACCOUNT — PROTECTION OF BUYER'S RIGHTS.** I understand this account may be sold or assigned by Sears to another creditor without further notice to me. If so, the notice below, which is required by Federal law, is intended to protect any claim or right I have against Sears.

NOTICE: ANY HOLDER OF THIS CONSUMER CREDIT CONTRACT IS SUBJECT TO ALL CLAIMS AND DEFENSES WHICH THE DEBTOR COULD ASSERT AGAINST THE SELLER OF THE GOODS OR SERVICES OBTAINED PURSUANT HERETO OR WITH THE PROCEEDS HEREOF. RECOVERY HEREUNDER BY THE DEBTOR SHALL NOT EXCEED AMOUNTS PAID BY THE DEBTOR HEREUNDER.

Errors or Inquiries on Monthly Statements.
**NOTICE: SEE ACCOMPANYING STATEMENT FOR IMPORTANT INFORMATION REGARDING YOUR RIGHTS TO DISPUTE BILLING ERRORS. NOTICE TO BUYER: DO NOT SIGN THIS AGREEMENT BEFORE YOU READ IT OR IF IT CONTAINS ANY BLANK SPACES. YOU ARE ENTITLED TO AN EXACT COPY OF THE PAPER YOU SIGN. YOU HAVE THE RIGHT TO PAY IN ADVANCE THE FULL AMOUNT DUE.
RECEIPT OF A COPY OF THIS AGREEMENT IS ACKNOWLEDGED.**

SEARS, ROEBUCK AND CO.   (By) _____

_____
(Customer's Signature)   (Date)

_____
(Address)

10897-051 Rev. 3/82
Illinois

CHECK YOUR UNDERSTANDING OF AGREEMENTS AND CONTRACTS

Choose the best answer to complete the following statements.

_____ **1.** When you see the words "annual finance charge," it means
   a. the weekly charge.
   b. the monthly charge.
   c. the yearly charge.

_____ **2.** If you pay your whole bill each month for items you have charged,
   a. you will not have to pay a finance charge.
   b. you still have to pay a finance charge.
   c. you still must make installment payments.

_____ **3.** Your monthly payments usually depend on
   a. the fixed amount you have agreed to pay.
   b. the interest rate.
   c. the amount of credit you are allowed.

_____ **4.** Installment payments are usually made
   a. monthly.
   b. weekly.
   c. yearly.

_____ **5.** A liability is a.
   a. type of agreement.
   b. legal responsibility.
   c. rent agreement.

_____ **6.** "This policy does not apply to sale merchandise" might be part of a statement in a
   a. dry cleaners.
   b. department store.
   c. car rental agency.

_____ **7.** A lease is a
   a. credit agreement.
   b. rent agreement.
   c. type of warranty.

_____ **8.** When you leave collateral for a debt, you
   a. agree to repay the loan.
   b. leave the property or the title to property with the lender.
   c. get another person to share the debt.

_____ **9.** When you are late with an installment payment, you are
   a. delinquent.
   b. co-maker.
   c. in agreement.

_____ **10.** Charge applications ask you
   a. your religion.
   b. your race.
   c. your annual salary.

Warranties

WORDS TO KNOW

adjustments   minor changes or repairs

authorized dealer   person licensed or trained to sell and service a particular product

free trial   an offer to try a product out before you decide to buy it and accept the terms of the warranty

full warranty   a guarantee to service, repair, or replace a product for a specified time at no cost to the purchaser. Damage resulting from careless use will not be covered.

guarantee   same as a warranty; legal promise

incidental or consequential damages   any damages resulting from the owner's carelessness

limited warranty   a guarantee to service, repair, or replace a product with the purchaser sharing some of the cost. Warranties usually cover defects in materials and workmanship, not careless use.

maintenance   everyday care

manufacturer   person who makes a product

prepaid   paid in advance; describes freight or postage paid by the buyer

purchaser   person who buys a product; consumer

refund   give back

repair   fix; make work

warranty   guarantee; legal promise

workmanship   how well something is put together

A warranty is the maker's promise that a product is well made. Warranties usually come with such things as cars, tools, appliances, machinery, and electronic equipment.

Every buyer needs to know how to read a warranty. Study the list of words above. It pays to know these words. You will find them in most warranties.

Reading a warranty

Smart shoppers read the warranties on the products they buy. The warranties tell them (1) the time period during which the manufacturer will repair, replace, or service a product, (2) whether or not they will have to pay for repairs or services, (3) who made a product, and (4) how to go about having that product repaired or replaced.

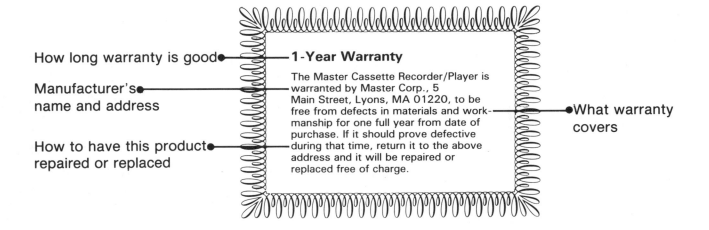

How long warranty is good •

Manufacturer's • name and address

How to have this product • repaired or replaced

1-Year Warranty

The Master Cassette Recorder/Player is warranted by Master Corp., 5 Main Street, Lyons, MA 01220, to be free from defects in materials and workmanship for one full year from date of purchase. If it should prove defective during that time, return it to the above address and it will be repaired or replaced free of charge.

• What warranty covers

Activity 5

Answer the questions about the warranty below.

Reading warranties for details

1-Year Limited Warranty

This quality Sharp CB equipment is warranted by Sharp Electronics Corp., 10 Keystone Place, Paramus, N.J. 07651, to be free from defects in workmanship and materials for one year from date of purchase. If it proves defective during that time, return it to the above address and it will be repaired or replaced free.

1. What is the name of the product under warranty? _____

_____

2. What's the name and address of the manufacturer? _____

_____

3. What does the warranty cover? _____

_____

4. How long is it good? _____

5. What do you do if this product doesn't work? _____

_____

Activity 6

Reading a car warranty

Every new car owner needs to know how to read a warranty. The warranty explains how to best service and maintain the new car. Car warranties also list what is covered and what *is not* covered. Some items will be covered only if a car is properly taken care of. Answer the questions about the following car warranty. The first set of questions deals with what *is* covered. The second set of questions deals with what *is not* covered.

1988 GENERAL MOTORS CORPORATION NEW CAR LIMITED WARRANTY

General Motors Corporation will provide for repairs to the vehicle during the warranty period in accordance with the following terms, conditions and limitations:

WHAT IS COVERED

REPAIRS COVERED
This warranty covers repairs to correct any malfunction occurring during the WARRANTY PERIOD resulting from defects in material or workmanship. Any required adjustments will be made during the BASIC COVERAGE period. New or remanufactured parts will be used.

WARRANTY PERIOD
The WARRANTY PERIOD for all coverages begins on the date the car is first delivered or put in use (as shown on the cover of this booklet). It ends at the expiration of the BASIC COVERAGE or other COVERAGES shown below.

BASIC COVERAGE
The complete vehicle, except tires, is covered for 12 months or 12,000 miles, whichever occurs first. Tire conditions caused by defects in material or workmanship of the vehicle are also covered during this period. The BASIC COVERAGE applies to all owners of the vehicle.

AIR CONDITIONING COVERAGE
The sealed refrigerant portion of the factory-installed air conditioning system is covered for 12 months, regardless of mileage. This coverage applies to all owners of the vehicle.

POWERTRAIN COVERAGE — 1st Owner Only
Following expiration of the BASIC COVERAGE, and subject to a $100 deductible, powertrain components are covered up to a total of 6 YEARS or 60,000 MILES, whichever occurs first. See pages 8-9 for a listing of parts covered, and details on coverage available to second and subsequent owners.

CORROSION (RUST-THROUGH) COVERAGE
Any body sheet metal panel that Rusts-Through due to corrosion is covered for 6 YEARS or 100,000 MILES, whichever occurs first. Sheet metal panels may be repaired or replaced. This coverage applies to all owners of the vehicle.

OBTAINING REPAIRS
To obtain warranty repairs, take the car to a Buick dealership within the WARRANTY PERIOD, present suitable identification to verify eligibility and request the needed repairs or adjustments. A reasonable time must be allowed for the dealership to perform necessary repairs.

NO CHARGE
Warranty repairs and adjustments (parts and/or labor) will be made at no charge (except for $100 POWERTRAIN COVERAGE deductible).

TOWING
Towing service, required if your vehicle is inoperative due to a warranted part malfunction, is covered to the nearest Buick dealership.

WARRANTY APPLIES
This warranty is for GM cars registered in the United States and normally operated in the United States or Canada.

(Cont'd. next page)

What is covered

Write the letter that best completes these statements about this warranty.

_____ 1. General Motors Corporation will provide for repairs to the vehicle
    a. as long as you own it.
    b. during the warranty period, without limitations.
    c. during the warranty period, with certain terms, conditions, and limitations.
    d. for six (6) years.

_____ 2. Repairs will be made by
    a. the General Motors Corporation.
    b. any mechanic you choose.
    c. the Buick dealer where you bought your car.
    d. any Buick dealer.

_____ 3. The basic coverage is for
    a. one year (12 months).
    b. 12,000 miles.
    c. one year or 12,000 miles, whichever you choose.
    d. one year or 12,000 miles, whichever comes first.

_____ 4. This warranty begins
    a. when the car is delivered to the dealer's showroom.
    b. when you pay your deposit on the car.
    c. the date your car is delivered to you.
    d. the date you decide on the car you want.

1988 GENERAL MOTORS CORPORATION NEW CAR LIMITED WARRANTY (Cont'd.)

WHAT IS NOT COVERED

TIRES
Tires are warranted by the tire maker. See separate tire warranty folder for details.

DAMAGE OR CORROSION DUE TO ACCIDENTS, MISUSE, OR ALTERATIONS
Accidents or damage caused by collision, fire, theft, freezing, vandalism, riot, explosion or from objects striking the car; misuse of the car such as driving over curbs, overloading, racing, or other competition; and alterations to the car. In addition, coverages do not apply if the odometer has stopped or been altered. Proper use is discussed in the Owner's Manual.

DAMAGE OR SURFACE CORROSION FROM ENVIRONMENT
Airborne fallout (chemicals, tree sap, etc.), stones, hail, earthquake, water or flood, windstorm, lightning, etc.

DAMAGE DUE TO LACK OF MAINTENANCE OR USE OF WRONG FUEL, OIL, OR LUBRICANTS
Lack of proper maintenance as described in the Maintenance Schedule; failure to follow Maintenance Schedule intervals; failure to use fuel, oil and lubricants recommended in the Owner's Manual. Proof of proper maintenance is your responsibility. Keep all receipts and make them available if questions arise about maintenance.

MAINTENANCE IS OWNER'S EXPENSE
Cleaning and polishing, lubricating, replacing filters, spark plugs and worn brake linings and performing other normal maintenance services all cars require. See Maintenance Schedule and Owner's Manual.

EXTRA EXPENSES
This warranty does not cover any economic loss including (without limitation), payment for the loss of time or pay, inconvenience, loss of vehicle use, vehicle rental expense, lodging bills, food, other travel costs, storage charges and other incidental or consequential loss or damage.*

OTHER TERMS: This warranty gives you specific legal rights and you may also have other rights which vary from state to state.

General Motors does not authorize any person to create for it any other obligation or liability in connection with these cars. ANY IMPLIED WARRANTY OF MERCHANTABILITY OR FITNESS FOR A PARTICULAR PURPOSE APPLICABLE TO THIS CAR IS LIMITED IN DURATION TO THE DURATION OF THIS WRITTEN WARRANTY. THE PERFORMANCE OF REPAIRS AND NEEDED ADJUSTMENTS IS THE EXCLUSIVE REMEDY UNDER THIS WRITTEN WARRANTY OR ANY IMPLIED WARRANTY. GENERAL MOTORS SHALL NOT BE LIABLE FOR INCIDENTAL OR CONSEQUENTIAL DAMAGES (FOR OTHER THAN INJURY TO THE PERSON) RESULTING FROM BREACH OF THIS WRITTEN WARRANTY OR ANY IMPLIED WARRANTY.

*Some states do not allow limitations on how long an implied warranty will last or the exclusion or limitation of incidental or consequential damages, so the above limitations or exclusions may not apply to you.

What is not covered   Answer these questions about this warranty.

1. Give three examples from this warranty of damages due to accidents, misuse, or alterations.

_____

_____

2. Give two examples from this warranty of damages from the environment.

_____

_____

3. Who pays for routine maintenance services? _____

_____

4. How will you know *when* your new car needs maintenance? _____

_____

_____

_____

CHECK YOUR UNDERSTANDING OF WARRANTIES

Choose the best answer to complete the following statements.

_____ **1.** "Incidental or consequential" damages describe
   a. defects in workmanship.
   b. defects in the materials.
   c. damage from careless use.

_____ **2.** When you send a defective product back to the manufacturer for a repair,
   a. you usually pay the postage.
   b. the manufacturer will pay the postage.
   c. the store where you bought it will pay the postage.

_____ **3.** "Damages resulting from workmanship" means
   a. you damaged it when you put it together.
   b. the product was not put together correctly at the factory.
   c. the product was incorrectly packed.

_____ **4.** The digital watch you purchased stopped working within one month of purchase. It is covered by a one-year warranty. You should
   a. send or take the watch to the place where you bought it.
   b. take the watch to a local jeweler for repair.
   c. read the warranty and send or take the watch to the place specified.

_____ **5.** The warranty on a new car begins
   a. when you order the car.
   b. ten days after you get the car.
   c. when the car is delivered to you.

_____ **6.** The tires on new cars are
   a. warranted by the tire maker.
   b. warranted by the automobile company.
   c. not covered by any warranty.

_____ **7.** You have owned your car for more than one year and have driven it 10,750 miles when it breaks down. Your dealer
   a. will charge you for repairs.
   b. will not charge you for repairs.
   c. will give you a discount on the repairs.

_____ **8.** If your car windshield is broken by a tree limb during a high wind and the car is under warranty,
   a. the car dealer will replace the windshield without charge.
   b. the car dealer will charge to replace the windshield.
   c. you will pay one-half of the cost of replacing the windshield.

_____ **9.** An authorized dealer is
   a. anyone who sells the product.
   b. a seller who is licensed by the manufacturer to sell and service the product.
   c. a repair service.

_____ **10.** Warranties usually cover
   a. any damage to a product during the time of the warranty.
   b. defects in workmanship and materials during the time of the warranty.
   c. defects in the product caused by heat or extreme cold.

Reference skills

Do you know how to find a book in a library card catalog? Do you know how useful a dictionary is? Do you use a book's index or table of contents when you need information quickly?

In this chapter you will learn about using the library. You will also practice dictionary skills and learn how to use tables of contents and indexes. All of these are reference skills. The first topic is using the library.

Using the library

WORDS TO KNOW

alphabetical   in the same order as the letters of the alphabet

call number   a number used by a library to identify a nonfiction book

call slip   a form for writing down the author, title, and call number of a book

card catalog   a collection of cards in drawers that lists the books in a library

circulation desk   the place in a library where books are checked in and out

closed shelves   parts of a library not open to users

cross reference   the suggestion of an additional source to examine

Dewey Decimal System   a system of classifying books by subjects

encyclopedia   a book or set of books that has articles on many subjects

fiction   a made-up story

general collection   the books in a library that circulate, not reference sets or magazines

nonfiction   a true report or account

numerical order   in order by numbers

periodical   something printed weekly or monthly but not daily, like a magazine

reference book   a book used to find facts or information quickly; examples are a dictionary or an encyclopedia

A library has three kinds of resources. One is the general collection. You may check out books from this group. The card catalog helps you find these books. To use the catalog you must learn the Dewey Decimal System. Another resource is the reference collection. It has dictionaries, encyclopedias, and more. You must use these books at the library. The third kind of resource is periodicals. The periodicals collection has pamphlets and magazines. You must also use these at the library.

The card catalog

Most libraries have a card catalog. It helps readers find the books they want.

All books in the library are listed in the card catalog. The card catalog helps identify and locate books. It is a series of drawers. The cards in each drawer are arranged alphabetically. The drawers are also arranged alphabetically. Each drawer has cards listing books in the library. You can find a book listed in the catalog by *author, title,* or *subject.*

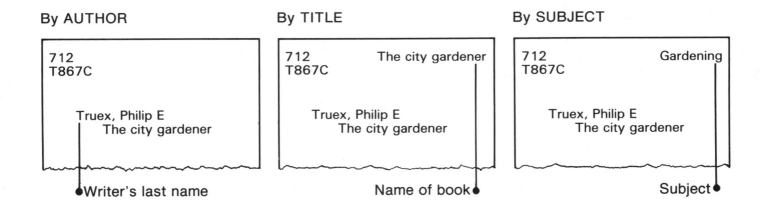

By AUTHOR

712
T867C

Truex, Philip E
    The city gardener

●Writer's last name

By TITLE

712   The city gardener
T867C

Truex, Philip E
    The city gardener

Name of book●

By SUBJECT

712   Gardening
T867C

Truex, Philip E
    The city gardener

Subject●

How do you find a book you want? There are several ways. You can look up the author's last name. You can look up the title of the book. Or you can look up the subject of a book. Author and title cards are often in one section of the card catalog. Subject cards are in their own section.

The three types of cards are shown on the next page. The book is Barry Green's *The Directory of Athletic Scholarships.*

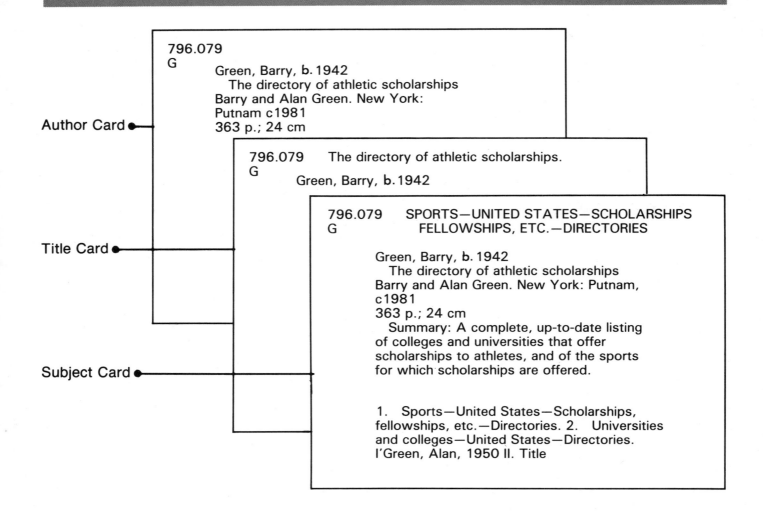

Author Card

796.079
G
    Green, Barry, b. 1942
      The directory of athletic scholarships
    Barry and Alan Green. New York:
    Putnam c1981
    363 p.; 24 cm

Title Card

796.079   The directory of athletic scholarships.
G
      Green, Barry, b. 1942

Subject Card

796.079   SPORTS—UNITED STATES—SCHOLARSHIPS
G   FELLOWSHIPS, ETC.—DIRECTORIES

    Green, Barry, b. 1942
      The directory of athletic scholarships
    Barry and Alan Green. New York: Putnam,
    c1981
    363 p.; 24 cm
      Summary: A complete, up-to-date listing
    of colleges and universities that offer
    scholarships to athletes, and of the sports
    for which scholarships are offered.

    1.   Sports—United States—Scholarships,
    fellowships, etc.—Directories. 2.   Universities
    and colleges—United States—Directories.
    I'Green, Alan, 1950 II. Title

When you find the card, you must note the "call number" from the card.

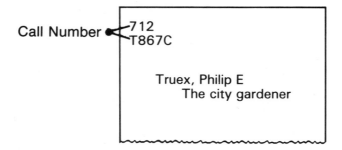

Call Number

712
T867C

    Truex, Philip E
      The city gardener

The call number on the author, title, and subject cards is the same. It is in the upper-left corner. This call number directs you to the book. Call numbers are based on the Dewey Decimal System of subject categories. See p. 36 for more information about the Dewey Decimal System. *The City Gardener* by Philip Truex has CALL NUMBER 712 T867C. This tells you that it is in the 700 section of the library. The 700 books are on the shelves in *numerical order*. You locate the books numbered 712. Then you find the books marked 712T. The T stands for the first letter of the author's last name. Your book should be among these. Books you check out are either fiction or nonfiction. Nonfiction books have a call number from 000 to 999. Fiction books, novels and short stories, do not have call numbers. They are put on the shelves alphabetically by the author's last name.

Today many libraries use computers to store information on their books. The information in the computer is the same as the information in a card catalog. Books are listed by author, title, and subject. Nonfiction books have call numbers.

Each library computer system has careful instructions on how to use it. Some systems ask you to use your skills at alphabetizing. You need to know how to put things in alphabetical order in order to find what you want. Other systems tell you to type in a name or a title or a subject. The computer's screen will tell you if the library has the book you want. It will give you the names of books on the subject you want. It will tell you the names of all the books the library has by one author. It will also tell you if the book is in the library or if it has been checked out.

Open and closed shelves

Most libraries let their readers get the books they want. This system is called open shelves. You get the book from the shelf and take it to the circulation desk. You then use your library card to check out the book. Sometimes someone who works at the library gets your book from the shelves. This system is called closed shelves. Many college libraries have closed shelves. If you use this type of library, you will have to fill out a call slip. This call slip will identify the book you want.

CALL NUMBER	PUBLIC LIBRARY **BOOK CALL SLIP** Author __Philip Truex__ Title __The City Gardener__	TEL. REQ.
712 T867C		

TO GET YOUR BOOK

1. Use separate slip for each book.
2. Take slip to shelves and search for book; if not found consult Librarian.
3. To get book from storage, present slip to call desk-
4. Your call slip will not be returned. Make a separate note of any information you may need later.

341-7/81
350M
A.O.S.P. X _____ d _____ XR _____ dR _____ DNR _____ NSL _____ TR _____ C _____ in use _____

Then take your call slip to the circulation desk. There, a library worker will get your book using the information you put on the slip. A library with open shelves may have some books that need a call slip. These might be rare or valuable books that need special care. A call slip may be needed to request these books.

Although most libraries use the *card* catalog system, some use *book* catalogs instead. They still use call numbers, but books are listed in catalogs, like large notebooks, instead of on cards. This system has *subject, author,* and *title* catalogs. These are arranged alphabetically, in sets, from A to Z.

Here are things you should keep in mind about the card catalog:

- Subjects that are persons' names are listed by last names. For example, on a subject card, Albert Einstein is listed as Einstein, Albert. The entry is on the top line.

- *A, an,* or *the* is ignored if it is the *first* word in a subject or title. On a title card, *The Scarlet Letter* is shown as *Scarlet Letter.* It is listed in the S drawer.

- Remember, there are *three* ways of finding a book. The book *Outline of History* by H. G. Wells is listed under:
    the *title* — *Outline of History* — in the O drawer
    the *author* — Wells, H. G. — in the W drawer
    the *subject* — History — in the H drawer

- Do not expect to find a call number for fiction works in the card catalog. To find a work of fiction, look for the shelves labeled Fiction. Then find the author's last name. The book will be in order by the author's last name.

Activity 1

Using the card catalog

Drawers of a library card catalog

A-Bl	Ch-D		Hi-K	N		Pi-Re	St-Ta
Bl-Bo	E-G		L	O-Pe		Ri-So	Te-U
Br-Ch	H-He		M	Pe-Pi		So-St	U-Z

You want books on the *subjects* listed below. Look at the drawing of the fronts of the drawers in a library card catalog. Which drawers will have cards on these subjects?

Drawer   **Drawer**

1. diesel engines   _____   11. art   _____

2. tropical fish   _____   12. magic   _____

3. Abraham Lincoln   _____   13. NATO   _____

4. Malcolm X   _____   14. hockey   _____

5. Albert Einstein   _____   15. macramé   _____

6. John F. Kennedy   _____   16. poetry   _____

7. photography   _____   17. music   _____

8. wrestling   _____   18. tennis   _____

9. boxing   _____   19. English literature _____

10. dance   _____   20. Yiddish   _____

You want books by the *authors* listed below. Which drawers will have cards on these authors?

Drawer   **Drawer**

1. Arna Bontemps   _____   11. Alex Haley   _____

2. Agatha Christie   _____   12. Walter Farley   _____

3. Simon J. Ortiz   _____   13. J. D. Salinger   _____

4. Judy Blume   _____   14. Madeleine L'Engle _____

5. James Baldwin   _____   15. Ray Bradbury   _____

6. Gwendolyn Brooks   _____   16. Robert Cormier   _____

7. Robert Louis Stevenson _____   17. Jules Verne   _____

8. Mark Twain   _____   18. Shirley Jackson   _____

9. Norma Fox Mazer   _____   19. John Knowles   _____

10. Walter Dean Myers   _____   20. Nat Hentoff   _____

The Dewey Decimal System

Libraries are divided into sections. Books on similar subjects are grouped together. This grouping is called the Dewey Decimal System. The call number on a book stands for the subject and helps locate the book. Here are the number categories in the Dewey Decimal System:

000-099	General works	500-599	Pure science
100-199	Philosophy	600-699	Useful arts
200-299	Religion	700-799	Fine arts
300-399	Social sciences	800-899	Literature
400-499	Philology	900-999	History

Each section is further divided into *ten* parts. Here are the ten parts of the 800's—Literature:

800	General literature	850	Italian literature
810	American literature	860	Spanish literature
820	English literature	870	Latin literature
830	German literature	880	Greek literature
840	French literature	890	Minor literatures

Each of these divisions is further divided. Here are the parts of the 820's—English literature:

821	English poetry	826	English letters
822	English drama	827	English satire
823	English fiction	828	English miscellany
824	English essays	829	Anglo-Saxon
825	English oratory		

Any further divisions are shown with a decimal. For example, a call number might be 821.09.

Some large libraries do not use the Dewey Decimal System. They use the Library of Congress System. Both systems have author, title, and subject cards. Both systems use call numbers. But the Library of Congress System also uses letters. Most libraries use the Dewey Decimal System. But some big-city libraries use the Library of Congress System. So the Library of Congress letter sections are shown for you.

The Library of Congress System, used by large libraries, divides books into lettered classes:

A	General works	M	Music
B	Philosophy—Religion	N	Fine arts
C	History—Auxiliary sciences	P	Language and
D	Foreign history and		literature
	topography	Q	Science
E-F	American history	R	Medicine
G	Geography—Anthropology	S	Agriculture
H	Social sciences	T	Technology
J	Political science	U	Military science
K	Law	V	Naval science
L	Education	Z	Bibliography—
			Library science

Activity 2

Using the Dewey Decimal System

Use the Dewey Decimal System to answer the questions below:

000-099	General works	500-599	Pure science
100-199	Philosophy	600-699	Useful arts
200-299	Religion	700-799	Fine arts
300-399	Social sciences	800-899	Literature
400-499	Philology	900-999	History

If you look for books on the topics listed, which call number section do *you* look in?

American literature_____

electrodes_____

the Civil War_____

British poets_____

nuclear energy_____

computer programming_____

cooking_____

travel_____

theatre_____

the Bible_____

U.S. Presidents_____

flowers_____

drug abuse_____

chemistry_____

Activity 3

Using a library directory

Use this library directory to answer the questions below.

Call number	Division of library	Floor
100s	Social Science/Philosophy	2
200s	History/Biography/Religion	2
300s	Social Science/Philosophy	2
400s	Language/Literature	1
500s	Science/Industry	2
600s	Science/Industry	2
700s	Art/Music	3
800s	Language/Literature	1
900s	History/Biography/Religion	2
Fiction	Language/Literature	1
B	History/Biography/Religion	2

1. On which floor are the 100s?_____

2. On which floor are the 300s?_____

3. What call numbers identify the books on philosophy?_____

4. What call numbers identify the books on language and literature?_____

5. On which floor(s) of this library are language and literature?_____

6. In which division of the library are the fiction books?_____

   the foreign language books?_____

7. What three subjects are in the 900s?_____

8. On which floor are books on science?_____

9. On which floor (or floors) are books with the call numbers below?

   901_____   811.08_____   629.13_____   759_____

10. What call numbers would be on books about World War II?_____

The Readers' Guide to Periodical Literature

Suppose you need a back issue of a magazine. Magazines are not listed in the card catalog. You may need to use the *Readers' Guide to Periodical Literature*. The *Readers' Guide* is a reference book. It will help you find the magazine you want.

In the front of the *Readers' Guide* is a list of the magazines that are in the guide. Here are some of the magazines that are in the *Readers' Guide*. Abbreviations are also listed.

Am Craft—American Craft
Am Educ—American Education
Bet Hom & Gard—Better Homes and Gardens
Black Enterprise—Black Enterprise
Car & Dr—Car and Driver
Consumer Rep—Consumer Reports
Cycle—Cycle
Dance Mag—Dance Magazine

Down Beat—Down Beat
Ebony—Ebony
Hi Fi—High Fidelity
Mech Illus—Mechanix Illustrated
Motor T—Motor Trend
Pop Electr—Popular Electronics
Pop Mech—Popular Mechanics
Roll Stone—Rolling Stone
Stereo R—Stereo Review
Work Wom—Working Woman

Here are some of the abbreviations used in the entries in the *Readers' Guide.*

J	January	Ag	August	int	interviewer
F	February	S	September	m	monthly
Mr	March	O	October	pt	part
Ap	April	N	November	v	volume
My	May	D	December	w	weekly
Je	June				
Jl	July	+	continued on later pages of same issue		
		por	portrait		
		il	illustrated		

Here is a sample entry from the March 1980-February 1981 *Readers' Guide.*

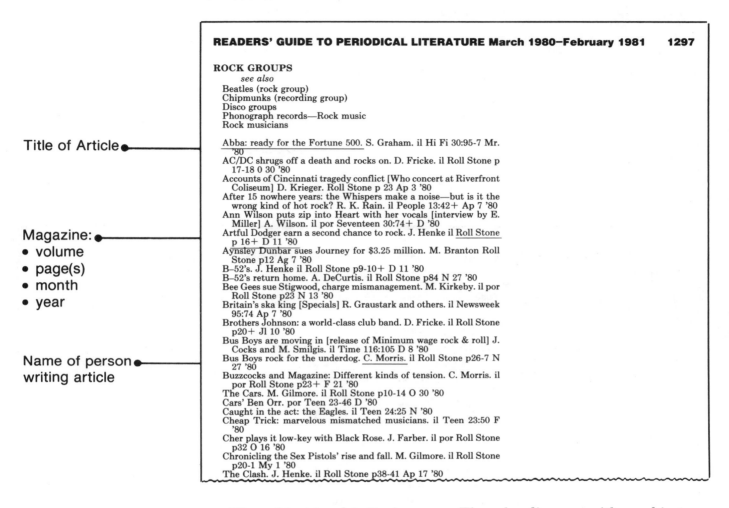

Title of Article

Magazine:
• volume
• page(s)
• month
• year

Name of person writing article

READERS' GUIDE TO PERIODICAL LITERATURE March 1980–February 1981   1297

ROCK GROUPS
   see also
Beatles (rock group)
Chipmunks (recording group)
Disco groups
Phonograph records—Rock music
Rock musicians

Abba: ready for the Fortune 500. S. Graham. il Hi Fi 30:95-7 Mr. '80
AC/DC shrugs off a death and rocks on. D. Fricke. il Roll Stone p 17-18 O 30 '80
Accounts of Cincinnati tragedy conflict [Who concert at Riverfront Coliseum] D. Krieger. Roll Stone p 23 Ap 3 '80
After 15 nowhere years: the Whispers make a noise—but is it the wrong kind of hot rock? R. K. Rain. il People 13:42+ Ap 7 '80
Ann Wilson puts zip into Heart with her vocals [interview by E. Miller] A. Wilson. il por Seventeen 30:74+ D '80
Artful Dodger earn a second chance to rock. J. Henke il Roll Stone p 16+ D 11 '80
Aynsley Dunbar sues Journey for $3.25 million. M. Branton Roll Stone p12 Ag 7 '80
B–52's. J. Henke il Roll Stone p9-10+ D 11 '80
B–52's return home. A. DeCurtis. il Roll Stone p84 N 27 '80
Bee Gees sue Stigwood, charge mismanagement. M. Kirkeby. il por Roll Stone p23 N 13 '80
Britain's ska king [Specials] R. Graustark and others. il Newsweek 95:74 Ap 7 '80
Brothers Johnson: a world-class club band. D. Fricke. il Roll Stone p20+ Jl 10 '80
Bus Boys are moving in [release of Minimum wage rock & roll] J. Cocks and M. Smilgis. il Time 116:105 D 8 '80
Bus Boys rock for the underdog. C. Morris. il Roll Stone p26-7 N 27 '80
Buzzcocks and Magazine: Different kinds of tension. C. Morris. il por Roll Stone p23+ F 21 '80
The Cars. M. Gilmore. il Roll Stone p10-14 O 30 '80
Cars' Ben Orr. por Teen 23-46 D '80
Caught in the act: the Eagles. il Teen 24:25 N '80
Cheap Trick: marvelous mismatched musicians. il Teen 23:50 F '80
Cher plays it low-key with Black Rose. J. Farber. il por Roll Stone p32 O 16 '80
Chronicling the Sex Pistols' rise and fall. M. Gilmore. il Roll Stone p20-1 My 1 '80
The Clash. J. Henke. il Roll Stone p38-41 Ap 17 '80

The subject head is Rock groups. These headings are either subjects or authors' names. They are alphabetical. The articles are listed under each subject heading. They are alphabetical by title. Notice that these articles were written in 1980-81.

Activity 4
Using the Readers' Guide

Study the sample entries from the *Readers' Guide to Periodical Literature.* Complete these statements about the entries.

1. The main heading includes cross references. A reader looking up rock groups could also look under other headings. List two other headings for information on rock groups._____

2. The title of the first article listed is _____

_____

3. The first article appears in what magazine? _____

4. An article titled, "Cheap Trick: Marvelous Mismatched Musicians," appeared in _____ in February, 1980.

5. "Bus Boys Rock for the Underdog" is the title of an article in _____ .

6. To find all of the articles on the Chipmunks, you must look under _____ .

7. Which magazine carried the most articles on rock groups? _____

CHECK YOUR UNDERSTANDING OF LIBRARY REFERENCE SKILLS

Rate your library reference skills. The statements below are about the library. Are these statements TRUE (T) or FALSE (F)?

_____ **1.** The *Readers' Guide to Periodical Literature* is a dictionary.

_____ **2.** The cards in the card catalog are always arranged by either author or title.

_____ **3.** Fiction books are arranged by the author's first name.

_____ **4.** Books within the 400s deal with literature and language.

_____ **5.** There are three types of cards in a card catalog.

_____ **6.** Nonfiction books do not have call numbers.

_____ **7.** The *Readers' Guide to Periodical Literature* is arranged alphabetically by authors and subjects.

_____ **8.** You can find books on a specific subject in the card catalog.

_____ **9.** Books with call numbers are arranged on shelves by the author's last name.

_____ **10.** You must know the author of a book to find the book in a library.

Dictionary skills

The *Readers' Guide to Periodical Literature* is a key reference book. Another important reference book is the dictionary.

A word can mean more than one thing. A dictionary gives you these meanings. The dictionary also tells you how to pronounce a word. And it gives you the part of speech of the word. Some dictionaries use a word in a sentence, too. This helps you understand the meaning. A word listed in a dictionary is called an entry.

Many people use the dictionary when they are not sure of a word's spelling. There are certain words that trip up even the best spellers: recommend, benefit, occasion. If you can't find a word in the dictionary, you may be misspelling it.

Synonyms and antonyms of words are given in some dictionaries as part of a definition. These help you understand a word's meaning. They also show you how a word can be used.

A synonym is a word that means the same or nearly the same as the entry word. A synonym for *sweet* is *sugary*. One of the meanings of *sweet* is a kind or pleasant disposition (pleasant person). A synonym for this meaning of *sweet* is *lovable*.

An antonym is a word that means the opposite of the entry word. An antonym for *clever* is *stupid*. One of the meanings of *clever* is "nimble with the hands or body." An antonym for this meaning of *clever* is *clumsy*.

Dictionary entries are in alphabetical order. Guide words help you locate a word. They are at the top of the page. Guide words give the first and last entries on a page. You decide whether the entry you want is between the guide words. Instead of *two* guide words to a page, some dictionaries use one. The guide word on the page to your left is the *first* entry on that page. The guide word on the page to your right is the *last* entry on that page. Study the following dictionary entry.

Guide words for first and last entries on this page.

Page number

a hat	i it	oi oil	ch child	a in about
ā age	ī ice	ou out	ng long	e in taken
ä far	o hot	u cup	sh she	ə = { i in pencil
e let	ō open	u̇ put	th thin	o in lemon
ē equal	ô order	ü rule	ŦH then	u in circus
ėr term			zh measure	

Key to pronunciation

Entries are arranged alphabetically.

pub lic ly (pub′lik lē), **1** in a public manner; openly. **2** by the public. *adverb.*

public opinion, opinion of the people in a country or community: *make a survey of public opinion.*

public school, 1 (in the United States) a free school maintained by taxes. **2** (in Great Britain) a private boarding school.

pub lish (pub′lish), **1** prepare and offer (a book, paper, map, or piece of music) for sale or distribution. **2** make publicly or generally known: *Don't publish the faults of your friends. verb.*

pub lish er (pub′li shər), person or company whose business is to produce and sell books, newspapers, or magazines: *Look at the bottom of the title page of this book for the publisher's name. noun.*

puck (puk), a rubber disk used in the game of ice hockey. *noun.*

puck er (puk′ər), **1** draw into wrinkles or irregular folds: *pucker one's brow, pucker cloth in sewing.* See picture. **2** wrinkle; irregular fold: *This coat does not fit; there are puckers at the shoulders.* **1** *verb,* **2** *noun.*

pud ding (pu̇d′ing), a soft, cooked food, usually sweet, such as rice pudding. *noun.*

Shows division into syllables.

pud dle (pud′l), **1** a small pool of water, especially dirty water: *a puddle of rain water.* **2** a small pool of any liquid: *a puddle of ink. noun.*

pudg y (puj′ē), short and fat or thick: *a child's pudgy hand. adjective,* **pudg i er, pudg i est.**

pueb lo (pweb′lō), an Indian village built of adobe and stone. There were once many pueblos in the southwestern part of the United States. *noun, plural* **pueb los.** [*Pueblo* comes from a Spanish word meaning both "village" and "people."]

Puer to Ri co (pwer′tō rē′kō), island in the eastern part of the West Indies, associated with the United States in foreign affairs, but ruling itself in local affairs.

puff (puf), **1** blow with short, quick blasts: *The bellows puffed on the fire.* **2** a short, quick blast: *A puff of wind blew my hat off.* **3** breathe quick and hard: *She puffed as she climbed the stairs.* **4** give out puffs; move with puffs: *The engine puffed out of the station.* **5** smoke: *puff a cigar.* **6** swell with air or pride: *puff out one's cheeks. He puffed out his chest when the teacher praised his work.* See picture. **7** act or process of swelling. **8** a soft, round mass: *a puff of cotton, a puff of hair.* **9** a small pad for putting powder on the skin. **10** light pastry filled with whipped cream, jam, or the like: *a cream puff.* **1,3-6** *verb,* **2,7-10** *noun.*

Definition

Word used in a sentence.

Pronunciation

puff y (puf′ē), **1** puffed out; swollen: *My eyes were puffy from crying.* **2** coming in puffs. *adjective,* **puff i er, puff i est.**

pug nose (pug′ nōz′), a short, turned-up nose.

Part of speech

42

Activity 5
Locating words in the dictionary

The words below are from columns of a dictionary. These words are no longer in alphabetical order. Arrange these words alphabetically.

Dictionary entries	Alphabetical arrangement	Dictionary entries	Alphabetical arrangement
complex	_____	possessed	_____
competitive	_____	possess	_____
complacency	_____	posse	_____
complacence	_____	position	_____
compete	_____	point	_____
competency	_____	postage	_____

Activity 6
Using guide words

Below is a list of words from three different pages of a dictionary. Then there are guide words from those pages. Put each word in the column where it belongs.

history	hogwash	hives
homework	hoax	hint
honey	honest	homage
horoscope	hole	horror
hostage	hotshot	hospital

hilt/hold   **holder/hooky**   **hooligan/houseboat**

_____   _____   _____

_____   _____   _____

_____   _____   _____

_____   _____   _____

Activity 7

Using the dictionary

Study the dictionary entry below. Then answer the questions about this entry.

puff (puf), **1** blow with short, quick blasts: *The bellows puffed on the fire.* **2** a short, quick blast: *A puff of wind blew my hat off.* **3** breathe quick and hard: *She puffed as she climbed the stairs.* **4** give out puffs; move with puffs: *The engine puffed out of the station.* **5** smoke: *puff a cigar.* **6** swell with air or pride: *puff out one's cheeks. He puffed out his chest when the teacher praised his work.* See picture. **7** act or process of swelling. **8** a soft, round mass: *a puff of cotton, a puff of hair.* **9** a small pad for putting powder on the skin. **10** light pastry filled with whipped cream, jam, or the like: *a cream puff.* 1,3-6 *verb,* 2,7-10 *noun.*
puff y (puf/ē), **1** puffed out; swollen: *My eyes were puffy from crying.* **2** coming in puffs. *adjective,*

1. How many definitions are given for the word "puff"?_____

2. Which definitions are for "puff" as a noun?_____ _____

3. Which definitions are for "puff" as a verb?_____ _____

4. Use definition #2 in a sentence of your own._____ _____

5. Is "puff" in definition #5 a noun or a verb?_____ _____

Activity 8

Using the dictionary to check spelling

Use your dictionary to check the correct spelling of the words below. One word in each pair is spelled correctly. Write out the correct spelling.

1. recommend, reccommend_____

2. accomodate, accommodate_____

3. accumulate, accummulate_____

4. occassion, occasion_____

5. personell, personnel_____

6. benefit, benifit_____

7. nineth, ninth_____

8. vaccuum, vacuum_____

9. omitted, omited_____

10. occurred, occured_____

11. committee, comittee_____

12. valueable, valuable_____

13. seperate, separate_____

14. arrangment, arrangement_____

CHECK YOUR UNDERSTANDING OF USING THE DICTIONARY

Use your dictionary skills to answer the following:

1. Put these words in alphabetical order. Pretend that any hyphens or spaces between words are not there when you alphabetize. In other words, arrange the words in order letter by letter.

drum major_____   double-cross_____

dose_____   donkey_____

doll_____   double_____

dope_____   doom_____

done_____   door_____

2. Study these guide words. Decide which ones should be at the top of the page for each of the words in the list below.

log/lollipop   Louis/love   lobe/locker

lounge_____   louse_____

locate_____   logger_____

logic_____   lobster_____

3. Use your dictionary to find the correct spelling for these words.

lisence/license_____   definitely/definately_____

hopeful/hopefull_____   privilege/privelege_____

comittment/commitment_____

45

Tables of contents

Do you use a book's table of contents? Do you use a magazine's contents page? The table of contents lists the subjects or topics with their page numbers. Unlike the index, this arrangement is not alphabetical. The contents page usually lists subjects in the order they appear. In this section you will study several tables of contents.

Books

A book's table of contents is usually arranged in chapters. Each chapter is numbered in order. Study the following partial contents page of a book. It shows chapters with subsections.

Contents

Chapter numbers

Chapter title

Page number for beginning of chapter

The subsections in this chapter

Activity 9

Using the table of contents of a book

This table of contents is divided into units. It also has sections. Use it to answer the questions below.

Table of Contents

v

1. How many units are there on this page?_____

2. What is the title of Unit One?_____

      Unit Two?_____

3. How many pages in this book are about Ralph J. Bunche? _____ Anne Sullivan Macy? _____

4. To which page would you turn to read about Martin Luther King, Jr.? ___ Leonard Bernstein? ___

5. If you wanted to read about courageous people, which unit would you read? _____

6. What is the name of *each unit*? _____

_____

Magazines

Is there a magazine that you read often? If so, its contents page is most likely easy for you to understand. Magazines usually list regular columns and feature stories in the table of contents. They also list their cover story. Look at this sample magazine contents page. These articles are listed in the order they appear in the magazine.

STARLOG PRESENTS

COMICS scene

ISSUE #1
JANUARY

Sometimes articles are grouped by subject. Sometimes they are listed in alphabetical order. Other times they are listed just as they appear in the magazine. Now scan titles of the items found in the magazine contents page just shown. Notice that the title of an article (or column) will clue you in to what it is about.

Most magazines have items that appear in every issue. These sections might be such things as Letters to the Editor or movie reviews or sports scores. The regular sections of a magazine depend on the general contents of the magazine. Sports magazines are likely to have regular sections listing schedules of games and scores. Beauty magazines would have regular sections on makeup and fashion. Often sections that appear every month are listed under the word *Departments* in a magazine contents page.

Activity 10

Using the table of contents of a magazine

On the next page you will find the contents page from an issue of *Ebony* magazine. Use the contents page to answer the questions below.

1. This issue contains a story about Pulitzer Prize-winning poet Rita Dove. On what page does the story appear? _____

2. Indicate whether the following items are in *Ebony* every month or are features for this month.

	Every month	This month
a. Bookshelf	_____	_____
b. Ebony Poll: Best Black Athletes	_____	_____
c. Space is Her Destination	_____	_____
d. Letters To The Editor	_____	_____
e. New Faces For TV's New Season	_____	_____

3. Is this table of contents arranged alphabetically, by subject groups, or by the order the articles appear in? _____

4. How many pages are there to the story about entertainers Jackson, Houston, and Baker? _____

5. On what page do you start reading about inventor Maurice Scales? _____

EBONY ®

OCTOBER 1987

VOL. XLII, NO. 12

INCORPORATING BLACK WORLD MAGAZINE

(ISSN 0012-9011)

CONTENTS

DEPARTMENTS

SUBSCRIPTIONS: One year (12 issues) $16. Two years (24 issues) $28. Three years (36-issues) $40. Canada
and Pan-American countries add $4 per year. Other foreign countries add $5 per year. Single copies $3.00.
Payable in U.S. Currency only. EBONY is indexed in the Reader's Guide to Periodical Literature. Member
Audit Bureau of Circulation.

Study the following textbook contents page. Notice that it has a number of divisions. Then answer the questions on page 52.

Contents

1. The contents page on page 224 shows two main divisions in the book. What are these two divisions? _____

2. Chapter 1 is divided into four subsections. What are they? _____

_____

3. On what page does the subsection called "Run-on Sentences" begin? _____

4. What is the title of Section 2? _____

5. How many pages are there in the subsection on "Making a Journal Entry"? _____

6. What can be found on page 51? _____

7. If you wanted to learn how to write a personal letter, what chapter would you read? _____

8. What is the title of Part 1? _____

9. How many divisions or subsections are there in Chapter 3? _____

10. How many chapters are there in Section 1? _____

Indexes

> **WORDS TO KNOW**
>
> **classification number**   the number of a section of classified ads, not a page number
>
> **index**   an alphabetical list used for finding information
>
> **subject**   the name of an item in an index, a topic
>
> **sub-topic or sub-entry**   an entry in an index that is secondary to the main topic, such as elementary schools under the main topic of schools
>
> **topic**   the name of an item in an index, a subject

A book index is in the back of the book. It lists words and topics alphabetically. It gives page numbers for these words and topics. This makes finding information easier. Most textbooks have an index. Look at the following book index.

Index

Notice the alphabetical arrangement of words, topics, and sub-topics. An index should list *every page* on which a word appears. Of course, not every word in a book appears in the index. Most often you find key words, special terms, and general topics.

Activity 11

Using a book index

Study the following book index and answer the questions about it.

Index

1. On what pages do you find complex sentences?_____

2. On what page will you find the word "couplet"?_____

3. How many pages does Chief Joseph appear on?_____

4. What pages deal with Jimmy Carter?_____

5. What page(s) should you turn to if you want to read about American Indian dances?_____

popular dances?_____

ballet?_____

Catalog indexes

Catalogs have indexes, too. A catalog index lists the items you can order. It also lists the pages where you can find these items.

Like all indexes, the catalog index is alphabetical. Most people use a catalog index when they want a certain item. For example, Bobby Goldstein wants to order a new basketball. He just got the mail-order catalog. Bobby turns to the index on p. 56. He looks under the B's for "Basketball." He finds "Basketballs" . . . 233.

Activity 12

Using a catalog index

Use the catalog index on page 56 to answer these questions:

• First, use the "Find-It-Fast Index" to complete the chart below:

Type of Product	Pages From	To
(1) Appliances	_____	_____
(2) Giftware	_____	_____
(3) Watches	_____	_____
(4) Tools	_____	_____
(5) Jewelry	_____	_____
(6) Home Entertainment	_____	_____

● Use the main index on the previous page to find the specific items below:

Item	Page(s)	Item	Page(s)
(7) Fondue Pots	_____	(14) Frying Pans	_____
(8) Drip Coffee Machines	_____	(15) Salad Bowls	_____
(9) Cookie Jars	_____	(16) Blenders	_____
(10) Humidifiers	_____	(17) Calculators	_____
(11) Electric Brooms	_____	(18) Movie Cameras	_____
(12) Clothes Hampers	_____	(19) Barbells	_____
(13) Fire Extinguishers	_____	(20) Ironing Boards	_____

Classified ad index

Another index is popular with shoppers. It's the classified ad index. As you may know, the classified section of the newspaper has many kinds of ads. Some ads are for jobs. Others are for buying and selling things. Still others list services. The index to the classifieds makes it easier to find the section you want. The index lists the ad divisions, or "classifications." It also gives a section or classification number.

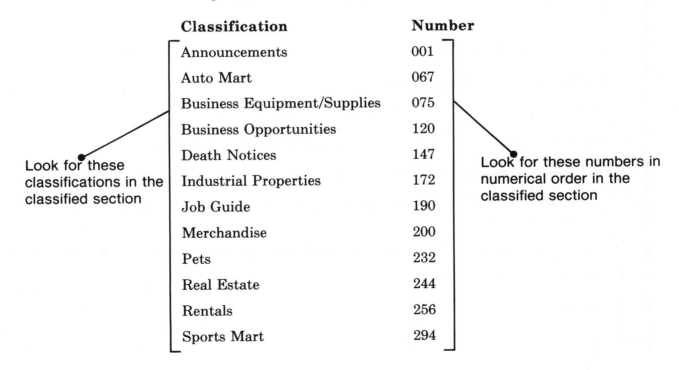

Classification	Number
Announcements	001
Auto Mart	067
Business Equipment/Supplies	075
Business Opportunities	120
Death Notices	147
Industrial Properties	172
Job Guide	190
Merchandise	200
Pets	232
Real Estate	244
Rentals	256
Sports Mart	294

Look for these classifications in the classified section

Look for these numbers in numerical order in the classified section

The number of sections you find in the classifieds will often depend on the size of the newspaper. Most classified sections have employment, announcements, merchandise, housing, and public notices.

CHECK YOUR UNDERSTANDING OF INDEXES

Use the following section from a classified ad index to complete these statements:

INDEX

The most popular classifications are listed in this index. Please refer to the Classified Pages for all classifications

ANNOUNCEMENTS
Classifications 001 to 023
Death Notices 001
Cemeteries, Monuments
 Crematoriums, Mausoleums ..003
In Memoriam........................004
Auctions..............................011
Personals, Personal Service .013
Attorneys, Legal Counsel.....014
Lost & Found 020
Transportation, Car Pools,
 Travel & Tours 022

Legal Notices 023
Entertainers............................044
EMPLOYMENT-EDUCATION
Classifications 024 to 045
Help Wanted 026
Help, Medical-Dental 027
Help, Office-Clerical 028
Help, Domestic.....................030
Help, Couples 031
Help, Sales 032
Situations Wtd.... **035,036,038**
Educational **039,041**

MERCHANDISE
Classifications 047 to 086
Trading Post..........................047
Sports Equipment 049
Diamonds, Gold, Jewelry 052
Miscellaneous for sale...........054
Flea Markets, Garage
 & Rummage Sales...........055
Cameras & Supplies.............058
Bicycles 061
Office Equip, Computers....062
Restaurant Equipment 064

Antiques, Collectibles..........066
Appliances...........................067
Furniture, Lamps, Rugs........070
Home Furnishings.................074
Moving, Storage
 & Mini-Storage 075
Stereo-Hi Fi, etc. 078
Television 079
Musical Instruments 080
Pianos, Organs.....................081
Building Materials 083
Machinery & Supplies..........086

TRANSPORTATION
Classifications 088 to 133
Autos for Sale...... **088 to 116**
Trucks, Trailers 118
Vans, Accessories..................119
Tires, Auto Access., Salvage .120
Recreation Vehicles...............126
Const. Equip., Mobile Offices
 Tractors, Farm Implements 127
Aircraft & Air Freight 128
Motorcycles, Mopeds
 & Mini Bikes 129

Boats, Motors.......................130
Sailboats 131
Performance Boats, Access. 132
Snowmobiles, ATVs 133
BUSINESS SERVICES
Classifications 172 to 228
PETS
Classifications 231 to 240
Horses, Livestock, Equip.......231
Pets-General 232
Tropical Fish & Accessories .233
Cats.....................................236

Dogs, Kennels.. 238
REAL ESTATE
Classifications 259 to 304
Real Estate Outside Detroit 269
Lake, River Property.... **271**
Florida Property,
 Sell-Buy-Rent-Lease..........273
Acreage, Sell-Buy 276
Comm. Bldgs., Land.. **280, 281**
Ind'l Bldgs., Land **281, 284**
Houses, East & West. **289, 291**
Condominiums, Co-ops.......292

1. The classification number for death notices is_____.

2. The classification number for auctions is_____.

3. The classification number for lost and found is_____.

4. The classifications mentioned in questions 1-3 are under the heading_____.

5. The classification numbers under pets run from_____to 240.

6. Today's Pets section contains five classifications. Complete the chart listing these classifications and their numbers.

Horses, Livestock, Equipment	231
Pets-General	
	233
Cats	
Dogs, Kennels	

ANSWER KEY

READING CRITICALLY

Activity 1, p. 3
Lose Fat Forever Ad
1. Answers will vary. 2. Answers will vary.

Career Certificate Ad
1. no 2. a box number 3. typing, auto mechanics, truck driving, hair styling, catering, barbering, computer programming, driver instructor training 4. Answers will vary. 5. a high school drop out; a high school graduate with no vocational skills; an adult who never attended high school
6. • When you finish the course . . .
   • Many people . . .
   • You don't have to worry . . .
   • The training is like college . . .

Activity 2, p. 6
1. **Intelligent Shoppers Ad:** b 2. **Hair color Magic Ad:** c

Activity 3, p. 6
1. Answers will vary.
2. • I know about *all cars* . . .
   • . . . what your car needs is PST.
   • . . . you'll run like a champion!
   • . . . it'll be ready for the Indiana 600 . . .
3. b (a is also acceptable)

Activity 4, p. 8
1. • Everyone, but everyone . . .
   • Get on the bandwagon!
   • Don't be the only one . . .
2. The drawing is of peole of all ages and occupations and of both sexes.
3. Answers will vary.

Activity 5, p. 9
1. Specific information 2. Glowing generality 3. Glowing generality 4. Specific information 5. Specific information
6. Glowing generality

Check Your Understanding, p. 10
1. guarantee 2. glowing generality 3. vanity 4. bandwagon appeal 5. optional 6. endorse 7. emotional appeal 8. glowing generality 9. lies and half-truths 10. sense appeal

Activity 6, p. 12
1. T 2. T 3. T 4. T 5. F

Activity 7, p. 13
1. 1¢
2. every four weeks; six times per year
3. nothing
4. indicate your preference on the card and mail it back by the date specified
5. 10 days
6. yes
7. yes
8. the buyer
9. $8.98 to $9.98; $4.98, $3.98, or $2.98; $14.98 to $15.98
10. after you have completed your membership agreement (to buy one more selection during the next year)

Activity 8, p. 15
1. four 2. $2 plus shipping and handling costs 3. 10 4. yes; there is a shipping and handling cost 5. 15 times a year (about every 3½ weeks) 6. four 7. mark the reply form and return it by the specified date

Activity 9, p. 16
1. Bold Hold hair spray; Cheerios cereal 2. Bold Hold; no; Cheerios; yes, 10 oz. or larger 3. no 4. Bold Hold: yes, 8/31/88; Cheerios: yes, 3/15/88

Check Your Understanding, p. 17
1. coupon 2. expiration date 3. obligation 4. refund
5. discount 6. redeem 7. T 8. T 9. T 10. F

UNDERSTANDING LEGAL DOCUMENTS

Activity 1, p. 20
1. installment 2. interest 3. percentage rate 4. disclosure
5. creditor 6. down payment 7. co-maker 8. default
9. delinquent 10. debts

Activity 2, p. 20
1. c 2. c (or a) 3. c 4. c

Activity 3, p. 21
A. 3 B. 2 C. 7 D. 8 E. 9 F. 1 G. 10 H. 6 I. 5 J. 4

Activity 4, p. 22
1. F 2. T 3. T 4. F 5. T 6. T 7. T 8. T 9. T 10. F

Check Your Understanding, p. 24
1. c 2. a 3. a 4. a 5. b 6. b 7. b 8. b 9. a 10. c

Activity 5, p. 26
1. Sharp CB 2. Sharp Electronics Corp., 10 Keystone Place, Paramus, NJ 07651 3. defects in workmanship and materials
4. one year 5. return it to the manufacturer at address on warranty

Activity 6, p. 27
What Is Covered
1. c
2. d
3. d
4. c
5. d

What Is Not Covered
1. Any combination of three of the following is acceptable: collision, fire, theft, freezing, vandalism, riot, explosion, objects striking the car, driving over curbs, overloading, racing or other competitions, alterations to the car
2. Any combination of two of the following is acceptable: airborne fallout (chemicals, tree sap, etc.), stones, hail, earthquake, water or flood, windstorm, lightning
3. the owner (buyer)
4. The Maintenance Schedule and Owner's Manual explain when maintenance is needed.

Check Your Understanding, p. 29
1. c 2. a 3. b 4. c 5. c 6. a 7. a 8. b 9. b 10. b

REFERENCE SKILLS

Activity 1, p. 34
Subjects
1. E-G 2. E-G 3. L 4. M 5. E-G 6. Hi-K 7. Pe-Pi
8. U-Z 9. Bl-Bo 10. Ch-D 11. A-Bl 12. M 13. N
14. Hi-K 15. M 16. Pi-Re 17. M 18. Te-U 19. L
20. U-Z

Authors
1. Bi-Bo 2. Br-Ch or Ch-D 3. O-Pe 4. A-Bl or Bl-Bo
5. A-Bl 6. Br-Ch 7. So-St or St-Ta 8. Te-U 9. M 10. M
11. H-He 12. E-G 13. Ri-So 14. L 15. Br-Ch
16. Ch-D 17. U-Z 18. Hi-K 19. Hi-K 20. H-He

Titles
1. Hi-K 2. E-G 3. O-Pe 4. A-Bl 5. Te-U 6. Ri-So
7. U-Z 8. N 9. Ch-D 10. A-Bl

Activity 2, p. 37

American literature 800-899
electrodes 500-599
the Civil War 900-999
British poets 800-899
nuclear energy 500-599

computer programming 000-099
chemistry 500-599

travel 000-099
theatre 700-799
the Bible 200-299
U.S. Presidents 900-999
flowers 500-599, 600-699, 700-799
drug abuse 300-399
cooking 600-699

Activity 3, p. 37

1. 2 2. 2 3. 100s, 300s 4. 400s, 800s, 5. 1
6. Language/Literature; Language/Literature 7. history, biography, and religion 8. 2 9. 901—2; 811.08—1; 629.13—2; 759—3 10. 900-999

Activity 4, p. 39

1. Any two of the following: Beatles, Chipmunks, Disco groups, Photograph records—Rock musicians
2. Abba: ready for the Fortune 500
3. Hi Fi (*High Fidelity*)
4. *Teen*
5. Roll Stone (*Rolling Stone*)
6. Chipmunks
7. *Rolling Stone*

Check Your Understanding, p. 40

1. F 2. F 3. F 4. T 5. T 6. F 7. T 8. T 9. F 10. F

Activity 5, p. 43

compete
competency
competitive
complacence
complacency
complex

point
position
posse
possess
possessed
postage

Activity 6, p. 43

hilt/hold	holder/hooky	hooligan/houseboat
history	homework	horoscope
hogwash	honey	hostage
hoax	honest	hotshot
hint	homage	horror
hives	hole	hospital

Activity 7, p. 44

1. ten 2. 2, 7-10 3. 1, 3-6 4. Sentences will vary. 5. a verb

Activity 8, p. 44

1. recommend 2. accommodate 3. accumulate 4. occasion
5. personnel 6. benefit 7. ninth 8. vacuum 9. omitted
10. occurred 11. committee 12. valuable 13. separate
14. arrangement

Check Your Understanding, p. 45

1. doll
done
donkey
doom
door
dope
dose
double
double-cross
drum major
2. lounge—Louis/ove, locate—lobe/locker, logic—log/lollipop, louse—Louis/love, logger—log/lollipop, lobster—lobe/locker
3. license, hopeful, commitment, definitely, privilege

Activity 9, p. 47

1. four 2. Courage Was Their Companion; "I Have a Dream"
3. 12; 11 4. 66; 118 5. Unit One (Courage Was Their Companion) 6. Courage Was Their Companion; "I Have a Dream"; Their Eyes Were on the Stars; Their Achievements May Surprise You

Activity 10, p. 49

1. 44
2. a. every month
   b. this month
   c. this month
   d. every month
   e. this month
3. by subject groups
4. 15
5. 51

Check Your Understanding, p. 51

1. Section 1 and Section 2 2. Using Vivid Words; Nouns and Verbs; Adjectives and Adverbs; Intensifiers 3. 28 4. Personal Writing: Writing for Yourself 5. two 6. Planning Your Life Story 7. Chapter 7 8. Let's Write! 9. six 10. four

Activity 11, p. 54

1. 237-239 2. 21 3. three 4. 89-91 5. 39-42; 36-38; 43-45

Activity 12, p. 55

"Find-It-Fast Index"
1. 154-174 2. 103-126 3. 80-93 4. 175-179 5. 4-79
6. 241-252

Main Index
7. 168 8. 160 9. 103 10. 173 11. 190, 191 12. 143, 224
13. back cover 14. 133, 134, 137, 158 15. 118 16. 167
17. 216-218, 250 18. 209 19. 235 20. 155

Check Your Understanding, p. 58

1. 001 2. 011 3. 020 4. Announcements 5. 231
6. Pets-General, 232; Tropical Fish & Accessories, 233; Cats, 236; Dogs, Kennels, 238